The Way Is Open

Other books by Glenn Martin

Stories/Reflections on experience
The Ten Thousand Things (2010)
Sustenance (2011)
To the Bush and Back to Business (2012)
The Big Story Falls Apart (2014)
The Quilt Approach: A Tasmanian Patchwork (2020)

Books on ethics and values
Human Values and Ethics in the Workplace (2010)
The Little Book of Ethics: A Human Values Approach (2011)
The Concise eBook of Ethics (2012)
A Foundation for Living Ethically (2020)
Future: The Spiritual Story of Humanity (2020)

Books on family history
A Modest Quest (2017)
They Went to Australia (2017)
The Search for Edward Lewis (2018)
All the Rivers Come Together: Tracing Family (2022)

Poetry collections
Flames in the Open (2007)
Love and Armour (2007)
Volume 4: I in the Stream (2017)
Volume 3: That Was Then: The Early Poems Project (2019)

Local histories
Places in the Bush: A History of Kyogle Shire (1988)
The Kyogle Public School Centenary Book (1995)

The Way Is Open

Glenn Martin

G.P. Martin Publishing

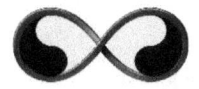

Published 2022 by G.P. Martin Publishing
Website: www.glennmartin.com.au
Contact: info@glennmartin.com.au

Copyright © Glenn Martin 2020
All rights reserved. No part of this publication may be reproduced or transmitted in any form or by any process without the prior written permission of the publisher, except for the inclusion of brief quotations for a review.
Glenn Martin asserts his moral rights as the author of this book.

Book layout and cover design by the author
Typeset in Palatino Linotype 11 pt
Printed by Lulu.com

Front cover: Picture and design by the author. The image is of the Temple of Literature, Hanoi, Vietnam.

ISBN: 978 0 6488433 6 8 (pbk.)

A catalogue record for this work is available from the National Library of Australia

Contents

Author Profile 1
Author's Preface 2
Part A: Young 5
    A roundabout trip 6
    Never get near the gate 7
    History of man 8
    Heaven must be here someplace 9
    Just enough 11
    After days 13
    Love and proximity 14
    The shape of sky 15
    This circus 16
    Your whole life 18
Part B: Living 19
    Accidental high 20
    Darklands 21
    The badlands 22
    Joy and sorrow 23
    Kookaburra (1) 25
    I live in the city 27
    Family history 29
    Science and the moon 30
    Pragmatist 31
    The labyrinth 32
    A recitation for meditation 33

- Articulating the crossing ... 34
- Truth in the midst of storms ... 35
- Kookaburra (2) ... 36

Part C: Firm Ground ... 37
- The handbook of Lu, the wanderer* ... 38
- Monk ... 39
- The dry well (Ching)* ... 40
- The reading ... 41
- K'un (Receptive)* ... 42
- The sage as stranger ... 43
- Ming I: Darkening of the light* ... 44
- Advancing in emptiness ... 45
- Olias* ... 46
- Waking to the moment ... 47
- Advancing ... 48
- The sage ... 49
- The old men have a saying ... 50
- In danger ... 51
- The sage's undertakings ... 52
- Kindling in the grate ... 53

Afterword ... 54

Author Profile

Glenn Martin (1950-) grew up in Sydney, Australia. As a young adult he left the city and ended up in a bush valley outside of Kyogle in northern New South Wales. He lived there for twenty years before coming back to Sydney. He has worked at many occupations: high school teacher, psychiatric nurse, community development worker, social researcher, and manager of community-sector organisations. Later he became a professional writer on management, employment law, training and development, and business ethics. He has been an editor of professional and academic publications. He has also been a lecturer in business ethics and human resource management, and an instructional designer for online tertiary education courses.

He is the father of five children, and he has four grandchildren.

Author's Preface

This collection contains poems from a broad sweep across my adult life. I started to see myself as a writer when I was aged nine, when I began to write small, rhyming verses. I liked being able to put words together in ways that entertained people and that accessed feelings. When I was eleven, I started recording my verses in an exercise book. I had some poems published in the (Sydney) *Sunday Herald's* Children's Page. And I had poems published at high school in the school's magazine, *Durian*.

However, I reached the end of high school with no idea of how to pursue life as a writer, so I opted for a utilitarian career as a high school teacher. Even in this I was thwarted, because my demonstrated knowledge was in Mathematics, not English, so I became a teacher of Mathematics. From there I moved on to other occupations, and writing had to occupy only small pockets of my life. I always had a day job; I fulfilled my financial responsibilities as an adult, husband and parent. But there was a dribble of poetry throughout the years, because for the making of poems you can create modest pockets of sufficient room.

I also learned to use words to articulate knowledge and construct arguments. I penned essays, reports, articles, papers, commentary, business plans and proposals, and I used these skills in my various jobs. There was a period of time when I lived at Kyogle when I wrote short stories too. While I was living there I was commissioned to write a history of the shire and a history of the public school (these were my first books), both of which were very well received.

I had gone to Kyogle in search of an alternative lifestyle. In a sense I achieved that for a while. It was certainly a place of retreat. But the more important gain was a developing sense of spirituality.

Eventually, when I was over fifty and back in Sydney, I put together my first collections of poems, selecting poems from right back to my early days – I keep all my poems in a large box (I was nurtured on paper, not bits and bytes). I did not seek a publisher, thinking that no one buys poetry books anyway, unless they are past masters like John Keats or T.S. Eliot, or Rabindranath Tagore. I published the books myself, and managed to sell a few copies.

In any case, I had started to write other books, particularly non-fiction books about ethics and human values. Later I added to this scope with books that I call "reflections on experience", which were a blend of personal life history and my evolving thoughts about life. And I had started exploring my family history, and that also led to books.

My work on ethics, which eventually culminated in a book called *A Foundation for Living Ethically*, helped me to formulate a perspective on life. Looking back, I can see how the ideas became clearer; it shows in my poems (well, it does to me). Thus, for this collection I have selected poems that fall into three developmental themes: "Young", "Living" and "Firm Ground".

The guiding light in all this has been the I Ching (or the Book of Changes), which calls one to be "steadfast and upright" amidst all the vagaries of life. I have been engaged with the I Ching (and the *Tao Te Ching*) for over four decades now. The goal of the practice is, I suppose, to be a master, a noble one, a sage. I say "I suppose" because truthfully there is no goal, only the present – to be attuned to all-that-is and to be in joy and correctness.

I apologise if the language may at times seem sexist. It is best to understand my use of the words as social conventions of the time the poems were written, that are intended to include everyone, accepting the historical limitations of language. One does not have scope for clumsy expressions in a poem; that is the province of legislation. The noble one, for example, in my mind may just as easily be a woman as a man.

This book is not the final word, but it is a milestone. I am conscious that even to say this is anachronistic; Australia had miles up until I was twenty-four, then it was all kilometres. My poems expose me several times with respect to technological changes. I see it merely as a lesson in the need for the constancy articulated in the I Ching.

Part A: Young

The only thing we did that was wrong
was to stay in the wilderness
for too long.

A roundabout trip

It's a roundabout trip,
learning to walk
two yards to mother's arms,
learning to talk in syllogisms,
acting in accordance with form.

I have known people
with springs and gear-wheels
inside their heads,
too many people,
people after the roundabout trip:

I-am-a-nine-to-five-man,
I-have-a-pretty-wife,
and-a-house,-car,-and-two-children.
Good-morning.
Good-evening.

I have seen the junk
accumulate around me
and I am crying out,
telling myself while I am still alive:
not here, not here, not here.

We have been so long in the dark
that even beauty is frightening.
Direction-blind we watch any spark
that could lead to our enlightening,
wanting to be strung out towards the mark,
and to see the distance tightening.

Let me not worship false gods.

Never get near the gate

Never get near the gate,
never get near the gate,
walk past a thousand times,
never get near the gate.

Never touch the light,
never touch the light,
see it only through the window,
never touch the light.

Walk on down the road,
walk on down the road,
nothing we ever did was right,
walk on down the road.

The larger shadows loom to take us.
What price oblivion?
God, father, maker of all
brick walls, barriers,
sound-proofed, multi-padlocked
secret-combination vaults,
holes in the ground,
forts and prison camps:
Who, who, who is the holy one?
I can never remember.

Never get near the gate,
never get near the gate.
What was the offer that you made us?
Never get near the gate.

History of man

You stoop with your eyes to the stars,
carve out songs in the hollow silence,
bend back, work, sweat, fear and love,
and at the end of the day
are collected into Abraham's bosom.

You segregate the world in rows of test-tubes,
write an equation for the universe,
observe, analyse, classify, hypothesise,
and live forever as the man who discovered atoms.

You strive for your seat in the train,
spin your own plastic cocoon,
pay bills, press buttons, obey rules, advance,
and hand your passport to
the automatically forgiving, computerised God.

Press Button B if no one answers.*

That statement doesn't make sense today, but when I wrote it (1969), in public telephones, you inserted your four pennies into a slot and then dialled the number. If someone answered you pressed Button A to allow the pennies to be taken into the machine; if no one answered, you pressed Button B to get your pennies back.

Heaven must be here someplace

"Heaven must be here someplace."
He said it, tramping along,
going down to the creek
near the old stone hut,
frost in the air
and the city a long way behind.

He said it, having time
to listen to the water bubbling,
time enough to have a plan
splash around in his head while the sun dried him.

"Heaven must be here someplace."
He wasn't even close,
was close only to the man
who was taking so long to die,
was thinking only of that painful passage
into dumbness. He said it,
somehow, in spite of being numbed,
his voice thin but hard,
in the face of all
the unfulfilled plans, the tumbling fall
from a dumb man's limp hands.
Said it: his voice coming
from far off, but lingering:

"Heaven must be here someplace."
He sat, thinking,
happiness is always in the past –
we recognise it afterwards.
And then we start again,

extract a promise from some girl
who happened to look our way twice,
and so we live,
rising and remembering,
false hopes and keepsakes.

"Heaven must be here someplace."
He said it, persistent.
Turn another stone, kiss the earth,
turn your face to the sun,
be as one, make
your second birth.
Eternally now, ecstatically, heaven.
Heaven, here, someplace.

Just enough

Honest the day is rising,
is quietly asking,
if there is any question
let it poke with gentle rays
into acquiescent dark.
If a rhythm is called for,
a sparkle is all that is needed
to measure the pulse
and your eyes may pound as they please.

At a touch we all discover
the secret hopes we had withheld –
discovery bathed in such great happiness,
afterwards we would call it ecstasy.

Sometimes, the earth is just soft enough
for pockets of fragility to persist
for just long enough
for us to wonder
that love is possible at all.
And then every day,
the clean face of honesty
shining for only a moment
shoots rays across the other side of space.
A day of saturation
would break you open,
split down the centre and see
if you would spill out love.

Beginning in the dark
we taste what the light would do,

hope and occasionally
stand defenceless,
tempting the fire-bright.

After days

After days and days
the sky was clear
and the sun that shone
did not remember pasts.
Purposes that had lain silently
awoke,
and knew how soon to seize
their means and ends.
Spirit touched the fuel of hearts
and came burning through,
the day moved
with true aim
from the mystery of source
to new heights.

Love and proximity

After dark and between showers of rain
when the phone ceases and the television is quiet
there is the chance to sleep
and if not, to plough down demons.

It is the hour when soothsayers peddle their trite
      catechisms
and somehow I know the transaction would be tawdry.

At these hours I go alone,
not as if I were an island,
but cognisant of the hordes I have seen
shipwrecked at daybreak
with their whisky and cigarettes
and embarrassing sentimentality –
yes, you will see, it is sentimentality.

I sail true, eyes sharp for the shadows of rocks
and the safe beacon of lighthouses,
ears sharp for waves upon shoals
and so I keep my hull safe
to sail into harbours –
love is not always proximate.

The shape of sky

I have pondered the shape of sky
poured down cracks between buildings,
leaning on trees,
a blank canvas for the sun,
a host for clouds.
I have seen the sky angular
and as the softest margin over far hills.
I ponder the shape of sky,
patient with the limits we set for it.

This circus

This circus of thoughts
that comes of reading –
what one man thinks of concepts
    (versus reality),
what one woman thinks of memory
(a fateful geology or
a fond but desperate grasp).
It is all accelerating, it is
a madman foaming at the mouth.
The writings of men and women
are a thousand beckoning mirrors,
in soft light and harsh light,
from above and below,
and you know, eventually,
you will have to drop the mirrors
and hazard the broken glass
and worse still,
the absence of illusions.

Look, and there is the sage
at your shoulder.
Bewilderment and fate
are now less compelling.
You stop, turn,
you read only to hear the voice
of the sage
who does not flatter you
and who does not doubt you.
You see there is a dance
between fate and the sage
and you mark the steps of the sage,

to be able to be nimble yourself.
So you learn dancing –
from concepts to memories that are released,
from the comfort of memory
to the beckoning of a new future,
you are not afraid to step forth.

In new moments you know
that you must bring only your faithful self
that knows only the present
and who is prepared to swim
with the current
if the goal is everything
and if everything is love.

Your whole life

The beginning: awareness,
seeing the world as all-that-is,
then, as
I and not-I
seeing all-that-is as
what is and what is becoming
(what may be)
then, seeing
what is desirable and what is not,
and wanting my own good, my own satisfaction
and seeing how I exist among others
who are located in the same way as I,
amidst all-that-is.

Resolving to know,
to live knowingly,
to delve into all the depths and dimensions
of all-that-is
and be satisfied
with the desire to be one with all
and so to know, to feel,
to act, to enjoy
in all the realms and circumstances
of each day,
to ask what is helpful,
what is steadfast and upright,
and see what is enough
and know that it is sublime and abundant.

Part B: Living

Look from the place
where we are all one,
carry the light into the day,
stay open in the heart.

Accidental high

Sometimes get so high –
moved by the infinite
walking
past dreams of laughter
at oddest times
going to a lecture
on how to keep your feet
on the ground
God shakes moments
I see behind
the world is paper thin
I see behind
Sometimes get so high
almost by accident
going to a lecture
Father-God is watching
from the verandah
us playing marbles
Magically it's alright again
us playing the Infinite
Marble Game
in God's lap
you are brown
and I am blue
the marbles are golden
and the angels are ecstatic
I go home
and write in my diary
"The Magic Accident"
and it's alright.

Darklands

A loss of power and opportunity
(he sustains his secret powers)
I dream, dream, that's all
Lose direction
(trying, trying all the time
to hold onto the way)
Out in the darklands,
remembering, remembering the light;
is it enough to know there is a light?
And I am reeling, reeling
while I am asking these questions,
I am remembering the light
but falling all the same

The badlands

Gather up your heart and hurry on:
do you sense the badlands around you?
Now you need to wear armour
and keep alert.

There will be small safe zones
where musicians can tame the evils,
but you must not stay there too long
or your strength will be sapped.

You are sick,
You are weak, confused:
It is the badlands; it is not the end.

Gather your heart and move,
Seek out the return of joy.

The essential truth lives,
heart shall be released
at its destination,
the feast prepared,
child protected,
the secrets declared,
time connected, ever.

Joy and sorrow

The other half is happiness,
time as full
as the meaning of a tree
which is a tree which is a tree

words fall away
to leave us inside and outside complete
There is ever so much
ahead
and struggles, lessons

I let go the future
here I
dwell in all fullness

sadness and joy pass
I take it
we are here
the horror, impossibility
of any hope
of any room to exist
in the simple integrity
of earth-flowing manhood

I am the ache
in the heart of all plunderers
but here too
I am
all love
a wedge driven into heaven
drunk on wild pure certainties

the other half is happiness
I am here in happiness
I grin like a fault
in the smooth face of illusions

(gentle should be
the fall into truth)

Kookaburra (1)

Every day the laughing bird has performed,
she and her mate in the gum tree branches,
taking it in turns and contemplating each other.

That is how it is,
two silhouettes in the early light
while I wrestle with implacable chores,
working my way through the stark
to find time for the dream
to get to start the dream
to make the joy, the art, the project;
it is the retreat from free rein
that I am accustomed to,
it is a battle of patience.

So I listen for another way,
a shorter cut
where I am emptied of petty burden,
where my painstaking, tortured limp
is visited by lightness
so I see it can all be different.

I look up at gnarled branches,
the glistening drapery of leaves,
the unapologetic rough string of bark
and remember that this was my first memory,
the grey, sprawling grace of gum trees
and the lesson –
just to drink in this cool embrace,
that this scenery is my natural home
before I have to be breadwinner, citizen,

expert, stalwart, conjurer, teacher, resource,
repository, leader, servant.
I have my natural state, my totem
whence comes my strength – it is
the laughing bird; this
in a foolish world.

I live in the city

I live in the city,
but at night I hear
the sound of the mopoke,
and in the morning the laugh
of kookaburras.

I live in the city,
but it is an abode.
I sojourn here.
I wonder about the people
who see it like a prison,
their eyes focused on a tiny square
of barred light,
hoping for Noah's dove
to bring them a branch
of olive
from some paradise
buttressed by remoteness.

I live in the city.
I admit that at night I hear
the sound of traffic and trains also.
But there is silence in between,
and it is the same silence.
I ask,
is it the traffic that is silent,
or the mopoke?
I burn a candle.
The flame is steady.
The flame burns
oxygen and travail equally.

Travail withers in the still burn
of wick in night's embrace.

It is the same light.

Family history

Beneath the silence, secrets,
things deemed too hard to say.
(Don't go out into the woods to play;
I can't tell you why, just obey.)

As children we could take this to be protection –
from danger, or sadness perhaps,
but we grew older and were never made wiser,
just at home with a false set of facts.

And the keepers of the secrets died,
carrying with them the comfort
that we were safe.
But I say we would have been better
in possession of the truth,
however grave.
There is something ground-worthy about truth,
you can stand on it,
as hard as it may be.
The first thing is having a place to stand
so I can learn how to stand up straight.

But again – soften, think –
this is how dark the woods were to them,
full of hungry souls and angry ghosts.
In dying they hoped to kill the secrets,
for us, to save us,
from danger, from sadness.

But I have dug up the bones
and cried all the tears that were necessary.
The monsters have departed.
It is okay. It is okay to go out and play.

Science and the moon

The wind before dawn
sweeps around the full moon's face.
I can tell she is holding out to be aloof
but the leaves tell me differently,
they are pulling her into their scurry,
disdaining her claim to be implacable,
though I know she will become pallid
as the dawn bleaches the sky.

But soon, soon again it is silent.
(The leaves are off dancing in distant trees.)
The fleeting blush of moon is a thing of doubt,
and I am beseeched once more to believe
in the science of molecules and matter.

Pragmatist

"Be pragmatic."

I have a new meaning for pragmatism –
staying in the centre,
alert to everything around,
experiencing stillness
where I can see distance
with utmost confidence.
This is what works.
Holding on to steadiness
amid voices and clatter,
myriad agendas,
contests of perceptions
built on old memories
of disenchantment.
So, so and so.
And now I am not
holding on,
I am adrift, afloat,
anchored in the sublime only.
At one with deep sadness,
all sadness,
and all joy.
I go
along the path,
lightly.

The labyrinth

In the labyrinth I learned
the sound of feet,
I learned
to put one foot
in front of the other.
The next step
is all the path gives you.
And looking up,
the people you see
heading in the opposite direction
may in fact be further ahead or behind.
I learned
that you need
to walk every step of the labyrinth
in order to get to the centre.
I learned pace –
when sometimes at every breath
you have to turn direction again
and sometimes
you walk for ages –
long, striding steps
until rhythm is natural,
but knowing always
that the path will turn
and turn again
until we arrive at the still centre
where new life bubbles up out of
nothingness – *prima materia*
to which I bring flesh,
and words to mark the journey.

A recitation for meditation

I breathe in, I breathe out.
Breathe in, breathe out.
I set the omens at the four corners of the hidden lands –
I set the omen of light before me,
I set the omen of darkness behind me,
I set the omen of thoughts and thinking to my left,
and the omen of feelings and emotion to my right.
I sit within the omens, where all light arises,
breathing in, and out.
I sit in the golden light,
and blue light surrounds me,
I am protected.
I am grace, I am energy, I am love.
I make a new day.
Wordless, I let go of the striving
to be eternal.
Here,
still,
I am older than the earth,
infinite,
and days will take their place.

Articulating the crossing

How well the moon takes the sky.
I walk the shining road
to banish cloying dark.
I am imbued,
I would call it new light,
I step nimbly
and turn away from gloom,
the ready companion.
I take the moon's glow
to roam. This is new.
This is as if first time:
I spurn the sad verses
and aspire to a clean connection,
the moment that rides high.
Thus I cross the fearsome plain:
in hand with shining moon,
walking the shining road.

Truth in the midst of storms

There are wild storms
and I see that I am travelling
in a strange land –
In a crass world I still carry my heart
as an offering,
I am looking
for deliverance
while the clash of thunder
grows louder, closer,
the rain on the roof
is a wall of sound

I have no weapons –
none that would withstand
the blast in any case –
I carry my heart in an open hand
and steel myself –
not to be weak,
not to be needy,
not to be pathetic
but knowing

that the essential truth
stands unprotected.

Kookaburra (2)

Kookaburra come look me this day.
No laughing, just look me.
One eye sideways.
My clothes line, his perch.
I say (no talking, just mind)
I been Australia long time,
mother and father, long way back.
Kookaburra, he still look me,
he no go.
I say, I grow roots down;
this home now,
nowhere else.

Next day I hear laughter in
old mother gum tree.
Two kookaburras.
That welcome call.
I stay now.

Part C: Firm Ground

I am not the master of the universe
but I come from bliss
and that way I serve all-that-is.

The handbook of Lu, the wanderer*

We are wanderers
despite the effort to be anchored in plans.
We are chosen to be in moments
we are unprepared for
just so we can learn to appreciate
that too, and that.

The wanderer learns not to presume,
not to depend on solidity
however solid it may seem.

We wander best
with simple rules:
To enjoy.
To act with correctness.
To be bold but polite.
To know stillness in movement.
It is grand.

In the I Ching there are sixty-four hexagrams. Each one has an image associated with it. The procession of images represents all the manifestations of the interactions of yin and yang in the universe (all-that-is). There are cycles — birth, growth, maturity, decay, death — and every ending leads to a new beginning. Lu is the fifty-sixth hexagram. Lu is the wanderer.

Monk

The sun rises over jigsaw of buildings,
this is a season benign but delicate,
breezes lilting across morning shadows,
with young women neatly attired and intent
on making the office in time.
Around the corner a throng of early risers chatters,
bound for leisure pursuits
in a jauntily painted bus.

Breathe in, breathe out, sip tea,
stretch for openness,
stretch for vast goals, or none whatever.
Recall the dreaming monks
in mountains who, day in, day out,
committed the silence to memory
and painted the cherry blossoms for eternity.
Breathe in the chatter, the eager expectation,
and out, again.

Quell the tempests and carry the smile.
Today the monk is travelling
to a crowded village.
He will be watching in the town square,
observing the crows cawing
on scrappy fences,
and the farmer straining
to haul the obstinate ox across the bridge.
He will repaint the canvas.

The dry well (Ching)*

Water being muddy
the well was abandoned;
dry progress followed.

The last miles at night,
wooden bridges on rough back roads —
then the neat bowl of light,
still and waiting;
coat hung on the door.

Then time for play:
the constant heart is established in joy,
solid at root beneath great trunks
but loose in the wind,
so much so that the crown sways
dangerously,
but he grins,
for his mother is the earth
and he shines
in the mystery of winning
the contest of wind with song.

---

* *In the I Ching, Ching is hexagram 48, The Well — a place of replenishment, the constant and pure source.*

The reading

The pathway to peacefulness
is possible:
through the door of good and evil it lies.
No matter how tightly
the rope has been strained.

Seek no path
but to watch the steps that you trace
and the spring will come,
will blossom
in new colours,
so it will be a new vision,
and storm will be calm again.

Let your only act be
the act of the heart
that knows us all as one,
the heart that loves herself
in all whom she encounters.

Across time, walls and strangeness
strive for us all to know
ourselves as one.

Holy, holy, holy,
peace on all paths,
blossoms in eternity.
Time without striving.
Wholly.

K'un (Receptive)*

The man comes quietly,
he speaks with his heart;
at the foot of the steps he says,
"Father, I am here,"
looks up and is
K'un, the Receptive.
To him the Father will speak;
he is a son of the Father
and the Father's good gifts
shower around him.
He does not seek bounty,
nor does he sit and wait for it,
but in following he finds his proper lord.
K'un is firm, steady, clear,
a reflector of the Divine Will;
here, and here again,
uncircumscribed by sorrow,
K'un is the unbound,
a dancer in the joy of the Lord.

---

* *In the I Ching, K'un is hexagram 2, Receptive – Earth, nourishing, yin. (Hexagram 1 is Creative, Heaven, yang.)*

The sage as stranger

He sees both the desire and its fulfilment,
he knows pain and he knows
its lessons,
he holds no grudge
against necessities.
When he speaks, his conversation is flavoured
sweetly, free of all guile.
He wanders again, a stranger,
walks into places
at delicate times
demanding honesty,
and suddenly is near
(and the world sees)
as the pandemonium clears
and the one spirit
now, in its power,
is.
He stands quietly,
obedient,
forever in command.

Ming I: Darkening of the light*

Ming I sees the wheel of his life,
clouds steer over the mountain,
as dark as a pit,
but the eternity of his actions
is in the issue of his sincerity:
the light of day is in his love.

Darkness fails to rule —
the proud prince falls in confusion
at his moment of triumph;
the land stirs again:
emptiness awaiting the light.

Ming I turns into the darkness, pure,
empty of false hopes;
he clings to joy like flame to wood:
it is the nature of evil to pass.

In the I Ching, Ming I is hexagram 36, Darkening of the Light – the sun has sunk below the earth.

Advancing in emptiness

He advances by enhancing what men see as inferior;
He reveres what men call emptiness.

This is why Jesus walked on water,
and as the Risen One
disappeared through walls.

Men say of a thing, it is lost,
but what is lost?
It is easily restored.

Such truths go on forever,
appearing, disappearing,
like the golden heart
of the sun through mist.

Like the chance ray of light,
the thread runs secure,
anchored from ship to shore.

Olias*

Olias never slept
for he watched over the sleeping,
Olias never wept
for he never lost sight of the sun.
Through men's darkness he said it again –
"Man's natural state is bliss."

Olias, a stranger, a speaker of truth,
was mocked by the knowing,
who jeered at his youth,
but Olias was ever-young,
children called him "Piper"
and sang his songs.

So to them he promised gladness
in carnivals and dreams.
To them he said, "Remember me",
and spun them tales of remembering,
of rivers and mountains
and fairy queens,
of star-flights and sailing
with the sun.

To those whose hearts were light
Olias gave free course,
and for the doubtful he danced
that they might not grow older
and sadden in the ways of the world.

Olias was a character created by Jon Anderson of the UK progressive-rock music group, Yes. Olias appeared in Jon's album "Olias of Sunhillow" (1976).

Waking to the moment

He treads carefully,
seeking the path through fear and anger.
In his advance his foot falls
on the tail of a snake
but his foot is firm
and the snake does not stir.

When there are only small gains to be made
he makes small gains
and admits the shortfalls of success
without envy.

In fatigue or confusion
he remembers his resolve
and finds again the union
of soul and purpose,
assured that the tangled courses
of whims, virtues and wonder
will manifest the One.

Wake to the moment, move higher,
abandon false dreams, false desire.
Flashes illumine the one course,
clear to the heart of the one source.

Advancing

How is it that the poor man advances?
By listening
and seeing with his heart.
When he meets with delay
he waits.
Anxiety is far from him –
he is still
like the candle that awaits the dawn.

When he is undecided
he asks what is correct,
his heart is prepared for misfortune
but the heavens open to guide him
and his way is secure.

If he is in need
abundance greets him on the road;
he laughs as he is made rich –
accepts the honour lightly
and continues to listen.

And sometimes the voice that comes
rolls soft and golden
like the breeze over forest leaves,
like the ten thousand things again one.

The sage

If the sage is needed he is brought forth,
he is led by the hand
into the dance of the young;
he is there melting awkwardness into grace,
letting false steps and laughter undress their hearts.
In the dance he sees
fortunes rise and fall,
he sees moments arise for correction
and time-lands he measures with silence.

High is the kite of youth
in crazy winds,
and teaching is best done with holiness.

The eyes of the sage are clear,
as he dances in the sureness of light.
What night can darken him?
The young lead him forth
into their dance;
time-lands he breaches
with mimes of the One.

The old men have a saying

They read from old books
but do not worship time;
caution they observe
in all their acts.
Who is inspired by their docility?
Soldiers, gypsies or timid men?

Not the timid —
these men know when to move
with flash and fire,
when the right touch will loosen
the spirit's desire;
in crying, laughing,
in silence and in speech
they cling to their inner strength.

What is it they teach
from their old books?
Correctness, and beauty.
The old men have a saying:
Love the One.

In danger

In danger his only protection
is his sincerity;
with confidence he approaches the disturbance,
fulfilling what is necessary
and retreating.

When he is not in demand
he returns to his home;
if you ask him what he does there
it will not seem important.
Perhaps he watches the birds
or puts straw on his garden.

You will hear the sage in hard times —
he is sharpened by adversity.
In victory he will storm through,
flanked, it would seem,
by a dragon horde,
intent on the last crushing blow.

But at once he will turn aside,
and pick his way back silently,
knowing sadness too in that hour.
And one knows
it is only the lesser man
who would stay to mock and plunder.

The sage's undertakings

If others did as the sage does
their undertakings would proceed
with harmony and excellence.
The sage does not fight with circumstance,
he restrains his wrath
and banishes his fear,
ruling himself with calmness.

He takes his rest
when the mountains withhold his progress;
he moves when the obstacles clear.
In the cast of the mountain's shadow
he does not pronounce doom
but nourishes the secret hope
that hides in the heart of all perils,
retaining his clarity and resilience always.

His silhouette merges with the hills,
a play of light and shadow
dancing in the mysteries of each moment;
effortless is his force.

Kindling in the grate

In the evening
he laid kindling in the grate,
paused in the wake of the day
and took brief comfort
in the thick yellow flame,
and so continued
to be invincible.

In the hush
of the candle's light
he finds the promise of the sun;
when all things have taken place
it will be
as before all things were begun.

And so he rests,
even inside actions:
and knows the balance,
the eternal satisfaction.

Do you hear him singing
in the morning?
He calls upon the mountain to move.
His violence is alarming,
he drives fear into those who hear him.

Afterword

Perhaps it is necessary to say a word about the title: "The Way Is Open". It is an expression found in both the I Ching and the *Tao Te Ching*. In our world of changes, sometimes the Way is open, and sometimes it is closed and one must be still and patient.

However, in a larger sense the Way is always open, because the Way expresses the nature of the universe (or all-that-is) and shows us how to live in accord with it, effortlessly.

> Some say that the Tao is nonsense;
> Others call it lofty but impractical.
> But to those who have looked inside themselves
> It makes perfect sense
> And to those who put it into practice,
> Its loftiness has roots that run deep.
>
> There are three treasures that I guard and hold dear:
> Simplicity, patience, compassion.
> Being simple in actions and thoughts
> You return to the source of being.
> Being patient with both friends and enemies,
> You accord with the way things are.
> Being compassionate with yourself
> You reconcile all beings in the world.

This is stanza 67 from the *Tao Te Ching*, mostly from Stephen Mitchell's version (Harper Perennial Modern Classics, New York, 2006).

www.ingramcontent.com/pod-product-compliance
Lightning Source LLC
LaVergne TN
LVHW051711080426
835511LV00017B/2857